MARGARET'S STORY

Sexual Abuse and Going to Court

by Deborah Anderson
and Martha Finne

Illustrated by Jeanette Swofford

Dillon Press, Inc. Minneapolis, Minnesota 55415

Special thanks to Judge Patrick W. Fitzgerald, Hennepin County District Court, Minneapolis, Minnesota, who has labored to make sure that child witnesses are protected from aggressive tactics

Illustrations courtesy of Hennepin County Medical Society Auxiliary, Inc.

Library of Congress Cataloging in Publication Data

Anderson, Deborah, 1946-
  Margaret's story.

  Summary: Describes the experiences of a young girl who is sexually abused by her neighbor and what happens when she seeks help.
  1. Child molesting—Juvenile literature. 2. Sexually abused children—Juvenile literature. [1. Child molesting 2. Child abuse] I. Finne, Martha. II. Title.
  HQ71.A54 1986   362.7'044   85-25417
  ISBN 0-87518-320-4

Dillon Press, Inc., 242 Portland Avenue South
Minneapolis, Minnesota 55415

Printed in the United States of America
  2 3 4 5 6 7 8 9 10 95 94 93 92 91 90 89 88 87

Contents

Margaret's Story

Once, I had to go to court. I was afraid, but I did it. Now, I'm glad I did.

I had to go to court because of Thomas. He's a man who lived across the street. Thomas used to be a friend to me and to the other kids. He let us play in his yard and in his house. But he's not there anymore.

One day in the summer I was in Thomas's house. Everyone else was outside. While I was there, Thomas put his hand in my shorts. He touched me on a private place on my body, my vagina. He wanted me to touch his penis, but I wouldn't. I felt very mixed up. I didn't feel right about it.

Thomas made me promise not to tell. He said, "Margaret, don't tell anyone. This is our secret. If you tell your mother and dad, they'll be very angry. So promise you won't tell!"

I wanted to get away from Thomas. I felt afraid of him. I said I wouldn't tell, but I felt I had done something very bad.

When I got home, Mom asked, "Did you have fun at Thomas's?" I didn't say anything.

Then Mom said again, "Did you have fun?" I couldn't talk but I started to cry.

"Did something happen at Thomas's?" Mom asked. "Margaret, tell me what happened!"

I cried more then. It was hard to tell. I used to like Thomas. But what he did made me feel bad. He said Mom would be angry, but I told her because she was so worried.

At first Mom looked mad. I thought she was mad at me. But she asked me to sit with her in her chair. She was crying a little, too.

Mom said, "Thomas knew it wasn't right to do that. We trusted Thomas, but there's something wrong with him. Honey, what he did is against the law. People call it sexual abuse. I'm very angry with him. But I'm not angry with you. I'm very glad you told me!"

We talked for a long time. Mom told

me that I didn't do anything wrong.
That made me feel better. She told me
that we had to call the police and report
Thomas for what he did. He needed to
be stopped, she said.

Mom called the police. Two officers
came to our house right away. I thought
they would wear uniforms, but they had
suits on. One was a man and one was a
woman. I talked with the woman and
told about Thomas again.

When Dad came home, I was in the
playroom. I heard Mom tell him about
Thomas. They both sounded so loud
and angry! I thought they were angry at
me, and I started to cry. Dad came into
the room. He picked me up.

"What's wrong?" Dad asked.

"You and Mom are mad at me," I said.

Dad said, "Oh, no, Margaret! I'm angry at Thomas for what he did, not at you! You were hurt, and that makes both of us angry." Then he hugged me.

Mom told Dad, my sister Alexandra, and me about the police. She said that they arrested Thomas and took him to the police station. He had to go to jail for a while, but then he came home again. The police and the judge told him not to scare me or even talk to me, she said. He would go to jail if he did. She said that Thomas lied to the police. He told the police he didn't do anything to me. But, he did.

Mom said to us, "The police told me that Margaret may have to go to court, unless Thomas tells them that he lied."

"Why didn't they keep Thomas in jail?" I asked. "You said he did something wrong."

Dad said, "The judge let Thomas out of jail because he said he wouldn't bother you or us. Before the police can keep Thomas in jail, a jury must say Thomas did something against the law."

"Why?" I asked.

"It's the rule, the law we have," Mom said. "A jury must decide. A jury is a group of people. In court they listen to what everyone says. Then they decide if the arrested person did something wrong."

"I know," I said. "I saw court on TV."

Dad said, "If we go to court, a lawyer will ask you to tell what happened. Then you tell the jury what Thomas did."

I felt scared. "I don't want to do that, Dad!" I said. "I don't want everyone to know. And Thomas might get angry. Could he get me?"

Mom said, "No. He can't hurt you in court, or ever again. But, if we go, we have at least three months to get ready. Maybe Thomas will decide to tell the truth. If we have to go to court to tell, it won't be until after Halloween.

"Now, we need a rest after this day. Let's go make dinner. Margaret, you can make pudding. We all need to settle down."

I made the pudding. After dinner, Mom, Dad, and Alexandra played cards with me.

The end of summer came, and school started. The leaves fell off the trees, and Halloween came. It's one of my favorite times. I was a scary monster with big hands and tricked everyone. I didn't go to Thomas's house for trick or treat.

I was still afraid of Thomas. He was still lying to the police. He didn't ever come near me or talk to me. Sometimes I would see him get into his car. I didn't like to think about what happened at his house.

One day at breakfast, Mom said, "A lady from the court is coming today. She said her name is Diane. She'll be here at three o'clock to talk to us, because it's almost time for court."

My stomach hurt all day. After school, I tried to hide in my room. But Alexandra came to get me at three o'clock. Through the window we watched a woman come to the door. Mom opened the door and talked to her. Then Mom called us.

The lady was smiling at me. "Hello, Margaret," she said. "My name is Diane." I couldn't say anything.

"I'm here to talk to you about Thomas. It might be hard for you to talk about him," Diane said, "but it's important. First of all, Margaret, you did the right thing when you told your Mom what Thomas did. I'd like to say some things to you about that and about court, too. Okay?"

"Okay," I said.

"Did you know that lots of children have this happen to them, both boys and girls?" Diane asked.

I shook my head. I didn't know that before. I didn't know it happened to lots of children.

Diane asked if I knew anything about going to court. I told her what Mom and Dad said about the jury. Diane said that was right.

"Are you afraid of Thomas?" Diane asked me.

"I didn't used to be, but now I am," I said.

"The police told Thomas he can't talk to you or scare you. Has he?" asked Diane. I shook my head no. "It will be that way in court, too. There will be people in court to keep you safe. Your Mom and Dad will be there, too."

I asked, "Will there be a lot of people in court?"

"I'm not sure how many. For sure there will be a judge, the people on the jury, a police officer, two lawyers, two or three helpers, and Thomas.

"We want to show you the place where court is held. Next week I'd like you and your Mom to come to my office downtown. You can meet Elizabeth, who is a lawyer who cares a lot about kids. After you talk with her, we'll see a courtroom. Does that sound okay?" asked Diane.

I shook my head yes. After a while

Diane left. She was nice.

The next Tuesday, I didn't go to school. Mom and I went to the courthouse. We went to see Diane first. She had games and toys in her office and drawings by children on her walls. I got to play while she talked to Mom about what would happen in court. I listened, too. Mom looked worried. I was, too.

Diane took us to meet the lawyer, Elizabeth. Elizabeth's office was nice, and she was friendly. She shook my hand and said, "I'm happy to meet you, Margaret." Then she said hello to Mom.

"Margaret, would you come to sit and talk with me over at that table?" asked Elizabeth.

"Okay," I said. I saw crayons and paper on the table. There was more paper on a stand next to the table.

Elizabeth asked me about my friends at school, and my sister, and if we had any pets. Then she asked, "Do you like to draw?"

"Yes!" I said. "Drawing is one of my favorite things to do."

Elizabeth said, "Will you draw a picture of the room you were in when Thomas touched you?"

"Okay," I said. While I drew I talked about Thomas.

After I drew my picture, Elizabeth talked to Mom and me about court.

"There's one important rule for you to remember, Margaret. You need to tell the truth about what Thomas did. If you can't remember something, say so. Do you think you can do that?"

"Yes, but I don't want to tell in front of other people. Who will be there?" I said.

"Let's go see the courtroom now. We can talk there," she said.

In the courtroom my stomach started to hurt. No one was there, but the room was so big! It looked like the one on TV. Elizabeth showed me where the jury would sit. I told Elizabeth I knew about the jury.

Then she showed me where the judge would sit. "The judge's job is to see that all the rules are followed. There are lots of rules, but the one you need to know is to tell the truth," she said.

Then Elizabeth said, "A police officer will be here too, to make sure you are safe and everyone else is safe."

Elizabeth also said Thomas would be there.

I felt scared. I had not seen Thomas up close since it happened last summer. I wondered if he would be mad at me.

Elizabeth asked, "Are you afraid of Thomas?"

"Yes," I said.

"Why?" she asked.

"Because he might get me. He might look angry and yell at me," I said.

Elizabeth said most children are afraid to tell in front of the person who abused them. That is why the police and judge are there. "I believe you, and the police believe you. It is important to tell the jury so they can decide who to believe. It's important to tell when someone does something wrong to you. It's scary, I know, but it's important."

"I know," I said. "Okay, I will tell in court."

Before I went home I got to sit in the judge's chair. It was high up. I could see everything in the courtroom. I sat in one of the jury chairs. Then I sat in the chair I would sit in when it was my turn. Elizabeth asked me some questions, just for practice. After that, she told us that court would be next week.

Mom and I went to Elizabeth's office on the day of court. Everyone was very busy when we got there. Some people were moving around or reading papers. Other people were talking to Elizabeth. She seemed to be in a big hurry. Mom and I saw Diane. She came to talk to us.

Diane said, "Everything is going well. The police have talked in court. A doctor did, too. Margaret, soon you will get to talk in court, and then your Mom will."

I went to sit on Mom's lap. Diane asked, "Are you nervous?"

"Yes," I said. "And my stomach hurts."

"I think we're both a little scared, Margaret," said Mom. "But we have to do our best to tell what happened. And remember, after this time, you don't have to tell anyone about it again, if you don't want to."

Mom and I sat for a long time in a special waiting room. We sat still and didn't talk much. Then, the door to the courtroom opened. Elizabeth came in and said, "Margaret, it's your turn to talk now."

My stomach hurt. I hugged Mom's neck tight and cried. Mom tried to get me to let go. "No. I can't! I don't want to!" I told them. I was really scared.

Elizabeth said she would ask the judge for a little time. While she was gone Mom hugged me and rocked me. She whispered that I was a brave girl, and said she knew I could do it, and she loved me a lot.

Finally, I was ready. Mom gave me
another big hug and a handkerchief in
case I needed to cry more. She had a
mixed-up look on her face when I left
with Elizabeth.

The courtroom was full of people! The
judge was high up in his chair. The
police officer was standing by the wall. I
saw the jury. I saw Dad sitting in the

back. He waved a little at me.

Thomas was sitting there, too. I was so scared I started to cry again.

A woman asked me to stand and raise my right hand. She said, "Do you promise to tell the truth, the whole truth, and nothing but the truth?"

I said, still crying a little, "Yes." Elizabeth and I did that on my visit to the courtroom. Then Elizabeth asked me some questions about Thomas. After that, I had to stand up and draw the room where Thomas did the touching. I talked while I drew. It was easier to do because Elizabeth and I had done this before. I told the truth about Thomas.

Another lawyer, the one sitting by Thomas, got to ask me some questions, too. He wasn't nice like Elizabeth. His questions were harder. I didn't get to practice with him. Sometimes I wasn't sure what he wanted to know. After that, I got to leave and go back to the waiting room.

We all went home after Mom had been in court, too. I was ready to go home. Talking in court was scary, but I was glad I did it. I was glad to not keep

inside me the secret Thomas wanted me to keep. Everyone said I was brave to tell in front of Thomas, even if I didn't look at him. It felt good to tell the truth, even if I was afraid.

The next day Elizabeth called on the telephone. She talked to me and told me the jury believed that I told the truth. Elizabeth said the judge would probably make Thomas stay in jail for a while because he lied about abusing me. Then Thomas might get treatment. That meant that people would help him learn that he shouldn't hurt children.

I am glad I told on Thomas in court. Sometimes, I am still kind of afraid when I think of it. Mom and Dad said when I feel that way, I should ask for a big hug and a little talk.

And I do.

Children and Sexual Abuse

Margaret's story is a true one. She didn't know about sexual abuse at first.
Because of what happened with Thomas, she learned what abuse is. But there are things that all children should learn about sexual abuse.

- You all have the right to be safe. No one has the right to hurt or sexually abuse you—not a stranger, and not someone you know.

- Children have private parts of their bodies. A girl's private parts are her chest, her buttocks, and her vagina, which is between her legs. A boy's private parts are his chest, his buttocks, and his penis, which is between his legs.

- Sometimes parents or guardians must touch your private parts. This might happen when you are sick or hurt or when you have gotten dirty. Also, doctors and nurses may have to touch a private part when you are getting a checkup. These are some good reasons for touching private parts.

No one has the right to touch you on your private parts without a good reason. No one has the right to make you touch anyone else's private parts. Without a good reason, no one has a right to make you take off clothes. And people have no right to show you their

private body parts. If they do any of
these things, it is sexual abuse.

- You can say, "No!" if someone wants
  to hurt or sexually abuse you.
  Margaret said, "No!" when Thomas
  wanted her to touch his penis.

- Often, people who sexually abuse
  children try to keep it a secret.
  Thomas asked Margaret not to tell.
  But Margaret told her mother what he
  did. It was hard to do, because she
  was afraid. Many children are afraid.
  Most children feel that they did
  something wrong. But, they did not.
  The person who abused them did.

- Sexual abuse is against the law. When children tell about abuse, sometimes they go to court to tell, just like Margaret did. And sometimes the person who abused a child and then lies goes to jail, just like Thomas did.

- Not all children who tell about sexual abuse go to court. Sometimes the person who abused them tells the truth. The person says he or she is sorry. Then the judge meets with the abuser and decides what to do.

- It's also important to know not all people who abuse children go to jail. Sometimes the judge sends the person to treatment. There, the person gets help. He or she learns not to hurt and abuse children anymore.

- Most people can be trusted, and do not hurt children. But when a child is sexually abused, it is often by a person the child knows. Margaret knew Thomas. Other people who could abuse children are neighbors, babysitters, teachers, scout leaders, parents, relatives, or just about anyone.

You have the right to be safe. No one has the right to abuse you, not even someone you know.

Places to Get Help

A child who is being sexually abused
needs to tell about it. Here are some
people and groups who can help.

The family: Your parents
Your aunt, uncle, or cousin
Grown-up brothers and sisters
A grandmother or grandfather

At school: A teacher
A social worker
A school nurse
A friend

**In the city
or town:** A police officer
A neighbor
Someone from Child
Protection Services
A doctor or nurse

Words to Know

abuse (uh·BYOOS)—behavior by an adult or older child that is harmful on purpose to a child, and is not an accident

arrested (uh·REST·ed)—taken to the police station and put in jail for a while because the police believe you broke a law

buttocks (BUT·uhks)—the part of people's bodies that they sit on

court (KORT)—here, a meeting with a judge and sometimes a jury, who decide when someone has broken the law

courthouse (KORT·howss)—a building where there are courtrooms

courtroom (KORT·room)—the room a judge and jury use when people go to court

jail (JAYL)—a place where people are kept away from other people. Some people who may have broken a law stay in jail for a short time. Other people who have gone to court and who did break laws must stay in jail longer

judge (JUHJ)—the person in charge of the court who sees that rules are obeyed and who decides what will happen to people who break laws

jury (JER·ee)—a group of six to twelve people who have to decide in court if someone broke a law

law (LAW)—rules that everyone must obey

lawyer (LOY·er)—a person who studies laws and helps people in court by speaking for them

penis (PEE·nis)—the part of a boy's or man's body that hangs down between his legs

private (PRY·vut)—belonging to one person or group only

secret (SEE·krit)—something that is not shown or told to another person

sexual abuse (SEK·shoo·ul uh·BYOOS)—behavior by adults or older children when they touch or look at a child's private parts like the penis, vagina, buttocks, or chest, for no reason, or when those persons force a child to touch another person's private parts

treatment (TREET·ment)—special help that people are given when they are ill. Treatment can make sick bodies well, or it can help people who abuse others or themselves learn new ways to act

uniform (YOO·nih·form)—clothes that are all alike

vagina (vuh·JY·nuh)—the part of a girl's or woman's body that is an opening between her legs

Note to Adults

This book, which deals with a child's testifying in court, was written so that other children can share this emotional experience. The story is based on an actual case.

Although we feel that this book will offer needed information to all children, we would especially recommend it to children who have reported abuse; to children who know of someone who has been abused and who need an understanding of their friend's experience; and, most importantly, to children who an adult suspects has been abused, but who is afraid to tell. It is our hope that an adult who recommends this book will talk with the child and discuss his or her feelings after reading the book together. By presenting solid information in a nonthreatening story form, we hope that a child's worst fears about the consequences of reporting abuse will be addressed.

If a Child Reports Abuse. . .

If a child reports abuse to you, here are some guidelines as to what you might do:

- **Believe the child**. Children rarely lie about abuse.

- **Be calm**. You might tell the child you are glad he or she told you about it, and that you know it is hard to talk about it.

- **Reassure the child**. Tell the child it's nót his or her fault.
- **Report the abuse**. Tell the child that you must report the incident to the police or to Child Protection Services. Say that the child may have to talk about the abuse to a police officer or social worker, too.
- **Thank the child for telling you**. Let the child know he or she can talk to you later about the incident as well, if he or she wants.
- **Explain the reasons for reporting the abuse.** Tell the child that reporting the incident is not done to punish the adult but to stop him or her from hurting other children.

About the Authors

Deborah Anderson, Executive Vice President of Responses, Inc., has helped establish programs to aid both children and adults whose lives have been touched by abuse and neglect. Deborah developed and directed a sexual assault services program for the Hennepin County (Minnesota) Attorney's Office, and created the conceptual basis for Illusion Theater's internationally acclaimed production, "Touch," which presents information on abuse to children. Deborah has worked with students, teachers, and school administrators regarding child abuse and neglect, and has been nationally recognized for her work in the area of children as victims or witnesses in court.

Martha Finne, Director of the Children's Division of Responses, Inc., joined that organization after directing a survey of Minneapolis school children entitled, "Child Abuse and Neglect: From the Perspectives of the Child," the basis for these books. She has worked as a child abuse consultant, speaking to parent groups and elementary school staffs regarding child abuse and its prevention. Her background includes a degree in social psychology, counseling at the Bridge for Runaway Youth, and volunteer experience working with both public schools and social service agencies.

About Responses, Inc.

Responses to End Abuse of Children, Inc. is a public nonprofit corporation which tries to coordinate programs in all segments of the community aimed at reducing family violence and child abuse and neglect. The organization works with both the private and public sectors to develop the most constructive responses to these problems.

In 1983 and 1984 Responses, Inc. conducted a survey of Minneapolis school children to assess the children's knowledge on various aspects of child abuse and neglect. The responses to the survey provided the framework for these Child Abuse books.